Courageous Virtue

A BIBLE STUDY
ON MORAL EXCELLENCE
FOR WOMEN

by Stacy Mitch

EMMAUS
ROAD
PUBLISHING

*Dedicated with love, devotion, and prayer to my daughter
Elizabeth Catherine—*

*May you always follow the heroic virtue of the
great biblical women and saints who have gone before us,
most especially Elizabeth, the mother of John the Baptist;
St. Catherine of Siena, Doctor of the Church;
and our most holy and blessed Mother Mary.*

Courageous Virtue

A BIBLE STUDY ON MORAL EXCELLENCE FOR WOMEN

by Stacy Mitch

EMMAUS ROAD PUBLISHING

Nihil Obstat
Rev. James Dunfee
Censor Librorum

Imprimatur ✠
Most Rev. Bishop Gilbert I. Sheldon, D.D., D.Min.

© 2000
Emmaus Road Publishing
All Rights Reserved.

Library of Congress catalog no. 00-109706

Published by
Emmaus Road Publishing
a division of Catholics United for the Faith
827 North Fourth Street
Steubenville, Ohio 43952
1-800-398-5470

Cover design and layout by
Beth Hart

Published in the United States of America
ISBN 0-931018-00-6

CONTENTS

ABBREVIATIONS

The Old Testament
Gen./Genesis
Ex./Exodus
Lev./Leviticus
Num./Numbers
Deut./Deuteronomy
Josh./Joshua
Judg./Judges
Ruth/Ruth
1 Sam./1 Samuel
2 Sam./2 Samuel
1 Kings/1 Kings
2 Kings/2 Kings
1 Chron./1 Chronicles
2 Chron./2 Chronicles
Ezra/Ezra
Neh./Nehemiah
Tob./Tobit
Jud./Judith
Esther/Esther
Job/Job
Ps./Psalms
Prov./Proverbs
Eccles./Ecclesiastes
Song/Song of Solomon
Wis./Wisdom
Sir./Sirach (Ecclesiasticus)
Is./Isaiah
Jer./Jeremiah
Lam./Lamentations

Bar./Baruch
Ezek./Ezekiel
Dan./Daniel
Hos./Hosea
Joel/Joel
Amos/Amos
Obad./Obadiah
Jon./Jonah
Mic./Micah
Nahum/Nahum
Hab./Habakkuk
Zeph./Zephaniah
Hag./Haggai
Zech./Zechariah
Mal./Malachi
1 Mac./1 Maccabees
2 Mac./2 Maccabees

The New Testament
Mt./Matthew
Mk./Mark
Lk./Luke
Jn./John
Acts/Acts of the Apostles
Rom./Romans
1 Cor./1 Corinthians
2 Cor./2 Corinthians
Gal./Galatians
Eph./Ephesians

Phil./Philippians
Col./Colossians
1 Thess./1 Thessalonians
2 Thess./2 Thessalonians
1 Tim./1 Timothy
2 Tim./2 Timothy
Tit./Titus
Philem./Philemon
Heb./Hebrews
Jas./James
1 Pet./1 Peter
2 Pet./2 Peter
1 Jn./1 John
2 Jn./2 John
3 Jn./3 John
Jude/Jude
Rev./Revelation (Apocalypse)

Catechism of the Catholic Church

Throughout the text, the *Catechism of the Catholic Church* (United States Catholic Conference—Libreria Editrice Vaticana, 1994, as revised in the 1997 Latin typical edition) will be cited simply as "Catechism."

How to Use This Study

This Bible study is designed to help women of all ages and walks of life learn more about the virtues and how they apply to our daily lives as Christians.

In this study, you will discover what the Word of God teaches us about the virtues. I have included introductions and some explanations along the way, as well as quotes from saints, popes, theologians, and philosophers, but the bulk of the work has been left up to you. At the end of each chapter is a suggested Bible verse to memorize.

This study is designed to be used by both individuals and groups. A leader's guide is included in the back of the book to help those leading a small group.

The tools needed for this Bible study are a Bible, a copy of the *Catechism of the Catholic Church*, a pen, and a teachable heart. The Bible translation used in this study is the Revised Standard Version, Catholic Edition (RSVCE). This is the translation used in the *Ignatius Bible* (Ignatius Press), which may be ordered by calling Benedictus Books toll-free at 1-888-316-2640, or by visiting your local Christian bookstore.

PREFACE

There are two very basic facts about the spiritual life that are true for every Christian. First, we are all called to be saints, and second, saints are made in the tedium of daily life.[1]

Each and every one of us, created and held in existence by our most loving God, is made for heaven. He has sacrificed His Son, Jesus Christ, to redeem the world, and He desires to save all of us (cf. 1 Tim. 2:4; 2 Pet. 3:9). It is our decision to accept this free gift.

We accept God's free gift of the divine life with an offering of our own. Our offering is to die to our selfishness and pride and become the person God created us to be. As we all know, selfishness is a difficult thing to overcome. It calls for a continual, daily effort on our part to transform our daily routine into a path to holiness.

The practice of heroic virtue is part of the path to the divine life. It is in practicing virtue that we lose our sinful selves and become more like Christ. This is how saints are made.

It is my prayer that this Bible study will help you learn more about the virtues, examine your practice of them, and, in the power of God's grace, live them out in a way that will bring glory, honor, and praise to Him and eternal life to you.

In writing this Bible study, I have become indebted to a few special people that deserve my recognition and thanks.

I would like to thank Leon Suprenant, Ann Recznik, Beth Hart, Brian Germann, Karyn O'Neel, Shannon Hughes, Earlene Crkvenac, and Liz Greene at Emmaus Road Publishing. Their expertise and heroic sacrifices for the kingdom of God make the publication and distribution of this Bible study possible.

---

[1] Even the martyrs were made in their daily struggles. The virtues cultivated in their daily lives enabled them to be heroic in the hour of martyrdom.

I would also like to thank the women in my Bible study: Pam Burton, Ann Connolly, Monica Stoutz, Maureen Suprenant, and Helen Valois. Their prayers, encouragement, and ideas have supported and contributed to the writing of this study. I am truly grateful for the blessing of your friendships.

I must express deep appreciation and thanks to my husband, Curtis, who is truly a walking Bible concordance. Without his gifts of time, encouragement, love, prayers, and editorial and theological expertise, this study would not have been written. I love you.

Finally, I thank our Mother Mary and Saints Elizabeth, Catherine, Teresa, Thérèse, Claire, Francis, Thomas, and Jerome, upon whose intercession I have constantly relied for help.

"The goal of a virtuous life is to become like God."[2]

---

[2] Saint Gregory of Nyssa, as quoted in Catechism, no. 1803.

Virtue Explained

"Therefore, brethren, be the more zealous
to confirm your call and election,
for if you do this you will never fall;
so there will be richly provided for you an entrance
into the eternal kingdom of our Lord and Savior Jesus Christ."
2 Peter 1:10-11

What is virtue? Go ahead and try to come up with a definition—and don't cheat by looking at the rest of this introduction!

I am willing to bet this was a difficult task for most—not because I think those who do Bible studies are unintelligent, but because I can't remember the last time I heard a meaningful definition of the term given in everyday circumstances. Most of us mistakenly think that the virtues are academic categories reserved for philosophers and theologians. However, the virtues are the basic stuff of the Christian moral life. The Catechism has defined virtue as "habitual and firm disposition to do good" (no. 1833).

The virtues help us habitually do what is good. They are the building blocks for Christian moral living. Accordingly, the Church has developed a theology of the virtues, building on what the ancients discovered through natural law and what God revealed through divine inspiration.

Catholic tradition recognizes four cardinal virtues that are also known as human, natural, or moral virtues. They are prudence (wisdom), justice, fortitude (courage), and temperance (self-control).[1] The moral virtues are gained through human efforts, and the natural purpose of the practice of these virtues is a good life. However, as Christians, the goal that we are striving for is not merely a good life here on earth, but rather eternal life in heaven. Therefore, God in His goodness has elevated the natural virtues by His grace (Catechism, no. 1810). The natural virtues (prudence, justice, fortitude, and temperance) practiced in the power of God's grace help us meet not only our natural good but our supernatural end—eternal bliss in heaven with God. As Pope Pius XI explains:

> [T]he supernatural order . . . not only does not in the least destroy the natural order, to which pertain the other rights mentioned, but elevates the natural and perfects it, each affording mutual aid to the other, and completing it in a manner proportioned to its respective nature and dignity. The reason is because both come from God, who cannot contradict Himself.[2]

In addition to the four cardinal virtues, there are three theological virtues: faith, hope, and love (charity). These virtues are "theological" because they are gifts that are given to us *by* God at Baptism, and their purpose is to lead us back *to*

---

[1] The word "cardinal" derives from the Latin, "*cardo*," and means "hinge." Thus the cardinal virtues are the virtues upon which the other moral virtues hinge. The four cardinal virtues are not the only natural virtues but rather the primary virtues under which all the others are grouped and classified. Some examples of other moral virtues include patience, humility, and gentleness.

[2] Pope Pius XI, Encyclical Letter On Christian Education *Divini Illius Magistri* (1929), no. 28.

God. God is the beginning, end, and motivation of these virtues. Our understanding and practice of them depend upon God's grace. Because these virtues exist in us solely through the goodness of God's grace, the only way for them to increase is by grace. We cannot earn more faith, hope, or love by our good deeds. In order for us to acquire more faith, hope, or love, we must ask God for them in prayer and frequent the sacraments, which are instruments of His grace. Like grace itself, they are pure gifts from the Lord. The only goal of the theological virtues is our supernatural happiness. The virtues are not simply philosophical constructs, but rather the habits and dispositions that help us reach eternal union with God. It is from this vantage point that understanding these virtues becomes an important and exciting task.

1. Virtue is not typically a topic of discussion. What do you think are some modern impressions and misconceptions about virtue? How have you understood the term, and how does that compare with the descriptions given in this introductory lesson?

_____

_____

_____

2. Virtue is a habit of goodness that embraces the entire being of a person. Philosopher Peter Kreeft writes that "[v]irtue is simply health of soul."[3] How is virtue "health of soul"?

_____

_____

---

[3] Peter Kreeft, *Back to Virtue* (San Francisco: Ignatius Press, 1992), 64.

3. We should love the virtues and the practice of them. According to Wisdom 8:7, what is the work of those who love righteousness? In what way is this work profitable?

_____

_____

4. Our model for virtuous behavior is Jesus. What do the following events and passages reveal to us about the standard of behavior established by Jesus during His life here on earth?

a. Luke 1:30-35 and 2:4-7

b. John 4:34

c. Matthew 22:36-40

How do you think these lessons apply to our own lives?

_____

_____

5. Because the practice of the virtues is the center of the moral life, it is not surprising that the Bible, the handbook of the moral life, is clear on their importance. How do the following passages explain to us the importance of living virtuous lives?

a. 2 Corinthians 7:1

b. 1 Thessalonians 5:8-10

c. 2 Timothy 4:7-8

d. Titus 2:11-14

> "I repeat, it is necessary that your foundation consist of more than prayer and contemplation. If you do not strive for the virtues and practice them, you will always be dwarfs. And, please God, it will be only a matter of not growing, for you already know that whoever does not increase decreases. I hold that love, where present, cannot possibly be content with remaining always the same."[4]
>
> Saint Teresa of Avila

6. Unfortunately, virtue is not always practiced. What do the following passages tell us are the consequences of failing to be virtuous?

a. Matthew 7:21-23

b. 1 Corinthians 9:24-27

c. Galatians 6:7-8

7. Read 1 Samuel 17:1-54, the story of David and Goliath.

---

[4] Saint Teresa of Avila, *The Interior Castle*, as translated in *The Collected Works of St. Teresa of Avila*, trans. Kieran Kavanaugh, O.C.D., and Otilio Redriguez, O.C.D. (Washinton: ICS Publications, 1980), vol. 2, 447.

a. How did David cultivate virtue in his life? How did this method prove beneficial?

_____

_____

b. What lesson can you take from this story and apply to your life in a practical way?

_____

_____

> "Our lives for the most part are made up of little things, and by these our character is to be tested. . . . Little duties carefully discharged; little temptations earnestly resisted with the strength God supplies; little sins crucified; these all together help to form that character which is to be described not as popular or glamorous, but as moral and noble."[5]
>
> Fulton J. Sheen

8. God has redeemed us through His Son's blood, and He has given us the grace of adoption to be His beloved children through Baptism. It is our responsibility to respond to this grace. According to Colossians 3:1-10, how are we to cultivate virtue in our lives and appropriately respond to God's great gift of life?

_____

_____

---

[5] Fulton J. Sheen, *Way to Inner Peace* (Greenwich, CT: Fawcett Publications, 1955), 15-16.

9. What has been your attitude toward studying the virtues? How do you think this attitude reflects the state of your spiritual life? During the coming week, pray for an increase of faith, hope, and love, and a desire to grow in the practice of the virtues.

_____

_____

_____

Memory Verse
"Therefore, brethren,
be the more zealous to confirm your call
and election, for if you do this you will never fall;
so there will be richly provided for you an entrance
into the eternal kingdom of our Lord
and Savior Jesus Christ."
2 Peter 1:10-11

Wisdom

"The simple believes everything,
but the prudent looks where he is going."
Proverbs 14:15

Pope John Paul II, while still a bishop in Poland, wrote a beautiful book entitled *Love and Responsibility*. In it he states:

Man's nature differs fundamentally from that of the animals. It includes the power of self-determination, based on reflection, and manifested in the fact that a man acts from choice. This power is called free will.[1]

The power of self-determination, to freely choose who we are and who we will become, is a gift from God. Not only is it a gift, but it is also a freedom and a responsibility. It is a freedom because it loosens us from the slavery of animal instinct, but it also requires us to take responsibility for our actions. No one is accountable for our actions or who we become but ourselves, because we are free to make our own decisions.

This freedom is demonstrated most notably in situations of tragic human duress like a Nazi concentration camp or a POW prison. These situations help to illustrate the sovereignty of an individual. In these situations, the torturers have chosen to be who they are and prisoners can choose how they react to their

---

[1] Karol Wojtyla (Pope John Paul II), *Love and Responsibility*, trans. H.T. Willetts (New York: Farrar, Straus, Giroux, 1981), 23-24.

torture. Heroes like Saint Maximilian Kolbe, who gave up his life for another in a concentration camp, refuse to be mastered by their aggressors or their own bodily passions and desires. They retain their God-given sovereignty to choose the good, no matter the personal cost.

Who we become is a matter of our own choices. In fact, our eternal destiny is contingent upon how we use our freedom. This is why the virtue of wisdom, which is the "perfected ability to make right decisions"[2] is so important.

1. Have you ever thought about your freedom to choose your own destiny and its importance?

Yes - mainly as it pertains to attaining heaven.

2. Wisdom is the virtue that helps us choose the ways and means of achieving our good. Wisdom is concerned with the means to our end. According to the following verses, what is our end? How does the theme expressed in these verses shed light on the need for the virtue of wisdom?

a. Matthew 16:24-27 *Heaven with God. Making right decisions is giving of oneself or self-sacrifice*

b. Matthew 25:31-46 *Wisdom needed in order to give generously to the poor, naked, hungry, thirsty, etc.*

c. Romans 14:10-12 *Do not judge others b/c you yourself will be judged is the theme here*

d. 2 Corinthians 5:10 *All people will meet Christ in judgement and will receive "good or evil" (heaven or hell) depending on what he or she has chosen to do in life*

---

[2] Josef Pieper, *The Four Cardinal Virtues* (Notre Dame, IN: University of Notre Dame Press, 1966), 6.

"In every good choice, as far as depends on us, our intention must be simple. I must consider only the end for which I am created, that is, for the praise of God our Lord and for the salvation of my soul. Hence, whatever I choose must help me to this end for which I am created."[3]

Saint Ignatius of Loyola

3. According to the world, how should we make decisions, and what should be our goals in life?

Our own advancement (ie, money, power, attractiveness, fame) is the world's main motivator of decisions.

How does this reflect the world's view of reality and of what is really important?

The world's view of reality ends with the physical death of the body.

Read the second chapter of the Old Testament Book of Wisdom. How does this chapter shed light on your previous answers?

It confirms that those who are "of the world" 1) see no afterlife or heaven and 2) see believing people as a "reproof" of their lives + choices

Explain why Wisdom 2 proves the old adage, "the more things change the more they stay the same."

Because in over 2000 years, non-believers still see believers as a personal attack to their lifestyle and lack of faith is common. Common,

[3] Saint Ignatius of Loyola, *The Spiritual Exercises of St. Ignatius*, trans. Louis J. Puhl, S.J. (Chicago: Loyola University Press, 1951), 71.

4. According to the following passages, what are the characteristics of one who is wise? Evaluate yourself according to the standards set in these verses.

The main characteristic of the wise here is:

a. Proverbs 14:8, 14-18

Caution and slow, thoughtful action

b. Proverbs 27:12

5. The virtue of wisdom is the cornerstone of the other virtues and helps lead us to heaven. According to the following verses, how is wisdom to be gained?

a. James 1:5 *Ask God for wisdom*

b. Proverbs 1:7 - *by first fearing the Lord meaning to know our place as creature*

c. Proverbs 2:3-5 - *by first desiring to fear God and to know Him*

d. Sirach 1:10 *Love God and then gain wisdom.*

6. According to these Scripture texts, who is the source of wisdom?

a. Proverbs 2:6 *the Lord - "His Mouth" gives knowledge + understanding*

b. Sirach 1:1, 9 *the Lord*

c. Wisdom 7:15 *God even corrects the wise*

7. In order to evaluate the best means to our end, we have to be able to see and understand reality clearly. We have to be able to see what is *really* real about the world, and only then can we make wise decisions as to how we should live. What do the following passages of Scripture tell us is the reality of this world and how we should live in it?

a. Matthew 7:13-14 *In this world, the easy choices that conform to the majority of others are not God's ways.*

b. Matthew 20:26-28 *Although it is human nature to seek self-advancement—this is not Jesus' way. He—God—came to serve.*

c. Matthew 6:24-33

A definite choice must be made by all men—either God or things. There is no middle ground.

8. Are there things in life and our modern world that skew reality and even make it difficult to see? How can we keep ourselves grounded in the truth about this world and God's kingdom?

One major problem is television and all mass media. Info. can be transmitted at such a fast pace and advertising can skew reality by portraying people and things that are false. Ads play on people's wants

9. For many of us, there is a gap between what we ought to do and what we actually do. True wisdom not only knows what to do but also follows through with the appropriate *+ make them more inflated.* actions. What do the following passages teach us about the importance of acting on what we know?

a. Romans 2:13 *Those who only hear the truth but don't act are not righteous.*

b. Galatians 6:7-10 *You will reap what you sow— You will get back what you give.*

c. James 1:22-25

You will be saved by your actions + works.

"But they are too attached to their honor. They would not want to do anything that was not really acceptable to men as well as to the Lord; great discretion and prudence. It is not always easy to reconcile these two, for the trouble is that without one's being aware the interests of the world almost always gain more than do those of God. These souls, for the most part, grieve over anything said against them. They do not embrace the cross but drag it along, and so it hurts and wearies them and breaks them to pieces. However, if the cross is loved, it is easy to bear; this is certain."[4]

Saint Teresa of Avila

10. Examine the virtue of wisdom in your life. Are you ordering your life and actions according to our ultimate end: heaven? Or are you trying to straddle the fence: attempting to have the "best of both worlds"—comfort in this one and heaven in the next? Jesus has warned us, "No one can serve two masters . . . You cannot serve God and mammon" (Mt. 6:24). In the Book of Revelation we are told:

> I know your works: you are neither cold nor hot. Would that you were cold or hot! So, because you are lukewarm, and neither cold nor hot, I will spew you out of my mouth (Rev. 3:15-16).

Quite frankly, I tremble at these words. What can you do in the next week to try to order your life according to God's priority for your life: salvation?

At times of temptation to yell at or be harsh with the children, I will stop and think "Jesus help me to get to heaven". To be quiet first and assess each situation.

---

[4] Saint Teresa of Avila, *Meditations on the Song of Songs*, as translated in *The Collected Works of St. Teresa of Avila*, vol. 2, 234.

Woman of Wisdom: Judith

The Book of Judith illustrates how God used the wisdom of Judith to deliver His people from an evil oppressor. King Nebuchadnezzar demanded to be worshipped as a god and sought the destruction of every city that disobeyed him. He sent out his army, under the command of his general, Holofernes, who had great success in crushing Nebuchadnezzar's enemies. Then the army approached the city of Bethulia, in Israel, which was inhabited by God's people. The Israelites, hearing the news of Holofernes' impending attack, fasted and prayed, seeking God's deliverance from the hand of their enemy. Meanwhile, Holofernes decided that the best way to defeat God's people would be an indirect attack. He ordered his army to surround the base of the mountain upon which the Israelites lived and cut off their water supply, forcing them to either surrender or die of thirst and starvation. The inhabitants suffered greatly and asked their leader, Uzziah, to surrender, reasoning that it would be better to be the slaves of Nebuchadnezzar than die such a horrendous death. Uzziah asked them to wait five more days for God's deliverance and after that he would surrender. However, God would deliver Israel through the wisdom and courage He gave a woman named Judith. Finish the story by reading Judith 8:4–14:5.

1. Uzziah praises Judith's wisdom in 8:28-29. How does he account for her great wisdom?

_____

_____

2. What is the first thing Judith does after she makes her plans to infiltrate the enemy camp in disguise?

_____

_____

28

3. What does Judith do in order to bring about the deliverance of the Israelites?

_____

_____

4. How does Judith instruct the Israelites to conquer the opposing army?

_____

_____

5. How was Judith an example of one who has wisdom? How was her wisdom acquired? How did she use her wisdom? What lesson from her life can you apply to your own?

_____

_____

_____

_____

═══════════ *Memory Verse* ═══════════
"If any of you lacks wisdom, let him ask God,
who gives to all men generously and without reproaching,
and it will be given him."
James 1:5

Justice

*"Blessed are they who observe justice,
who do righteousness at all times!"*
Psalm 106:3

I still remember a newscast I saw a few years ago about a crime so heinous that I refuse to write about it here, and for which the assailant received eighteen months in prison. I remember the story because I was shocked by the severity of the crime and the poor treatment of the accused. Both were examples of injustice.

Practicing the virtue of justice means habitually giving to another person what is due. A just person, for example, returns borrowed items, pays their bills in full, obeys God, and is polite and respectful to other people. These are the ordinary duties of all respectable people.

As Christians, the virtue of justice, elevated by God's grace, enables us to go beyond the minimal call of duty and actually enter into the heroic practice of this virtue. As Christians we practice the virtue of justice by acting toward others and God as He desires.

When we practice the virtue of justice, we presuppose that we actually owe someone something—like respect, courtesy, or honesty. It is noteworthy that we, as a people, have asserted in our Declaration of Independence and established as law in our Constitution that human beings, in particular, U.S. citizens, have certain "inalienable" rights. Inalienable rights, however, were not a concept invented by our Founding Fathers, but rather an endowment given us by our Creator. These rights, which include the right to life, religious freedom, and a fair wage for one's labors, have their origin in God, and were conferred upon us when He created us in His image.

Because these rights originate with God and are given us because we are made in His image, it logically follows that God also has rights. Therefore, justice is owed both to the Creator and to those who have been created with God-given rights. The Catechism (no. 1807) defines justice as

> the moral virtue that consists in the constant and firm will to give their due to God and neighbor. . . . The just man, often mentioned in the Sacred Scriptures, is distinguished by habitual right thinking and the uprightness of his conduct toward his neighbor.

1. Consider our society for a moment. Does our country and justice system protect and uphold the inalienable rights (e.g., the right to life) given us by God?

No - the widespread practice of abortion - euthanasia - contraception are examples

In what ways has this system succeeded or failed in protecting these rights?

Some social programs do respect people but some don't - Welfare is a good example of attempting to help but could end up hurting.

Do you think that any failures in the practices of the justice system stem from an uncertainty about what justice is and what is "due" our fellow human beings?

Often people mistakenly think of justice as "equality" of outcome. However, we know that God has given us all different gifts + talents,

2. The concept of justice presupposes that others have rights. According to Genesis 1:26-30, what is the origin of human rights and dignity?

Creation by God in His image + likeness is the origin.

> "Nevertheless, to praise you is the desire of man, a little piece of your creation. You stir man to take pleasure in praising you, because you have made us for yourself, and our heart is restless until it rests in you."[1]
>
> Saint Augustine

3. In the New Covenant, Jesus established the standard of justice for Christians. According to the following verses, how are we to treat our neighbors? How does this treatment differ from how justice would be practiced on a natural level or without grace?

Jesus goes 1 further than the OT - do not

a. Matthew 5:21-22 *Kill your brother but also do not even be angry or demean him.*

b. Matthew 5:38-42 *Do not resist evil" ⟹ Give more than those who ask you - This actually contradicts "An eye for an eye"*

c. Romans 13:7-10 *Love your neighbor as yourself - without grace, we would be unable to see past our desires + selfishness.*

> "When I act and think with charity, I feel it is Jesus who works within me. The closer I am united with Him, the more I love all the other dwellers in Carmel. If I want this love to grow deeper and the devil tries to show me the faults of a sister, I

---

[1] Saint Augustine, *Confessions*, trans. Henry Chadwick (New York: Oxford University Press, 1992), 3.

hasten to think of all her virtues and of how good her intentions are. I tell myself that though I have seen her commit a sin, she may very well have won many spiritual victories of which I know nothing because of her humility. What seems a fault to me may very well be an act of virtue because of the intention behind it."[2]

Saint Thérèse of Lisieux

4. What are some common situations that challenge us to live out Jesus' standards of justice? What are some practical ways to handle these situations according to Christian principles of justice?

A common situation is an occasion women often have to gossip. This is unjust b/c it "steals" a person's reputation. To avoid people who gossip or to change the subject.

5. God, our Creator and Father, has rights. According to the following passages, what do we owe Our Heavenly Father? How can we pay this debt in practical ways? Complete the following chart.

	What do we owe God?	How do we pay our debt?
Matthew 6:24 *No serve 2 masters*	*Our primary priority is God in all things*	*Praying 1st each day - Praying in tempting situations*
Mark 12:32-33		*By having an internal disposition that is holy not outward acts.*
1 Samuel 15:22	*to hear his voice & obey*	*Do his will not perform rel. acts*

It's Better to obey than offer sacrifices

[2] Saint Thérèse of Lisieux, *The Story of a Soul*, trans. John Beevers (New York: Image Books, 1989), 123.

"In taking account of us, He is not at all petty, but generous. However great our debt may be, He finds it easy to pardon; but when there is a question of His repaying us, He's so careful that you need have no fear. Just the raising of our eyes in remembrance of Him will have its reward."[3]

Saint Teresa of Avila

6. Because of our failure to render to God what is His due, namely, our worship, obedience, and undivided hearts, we needed to be reconciled to Him. We had a debt that needed to be paid before we could enjoy friendship with God. How has God reconciled us to Himself?

a. John 3:16 *By sending Jesus to die + so, conquering death*

b. 2 Corinthians 5:18-21 *By making Jesus "to be Sin" and so, we may become righteous.*

c. Romans 5:18-19

As Adam's one sin made us all sinners - Jesus' one self-giving act made us all able to receive heaven.

7. Reflect upon the message of our salvation described in the verses studied in the previous question.

a. According to Genesis 3:1-7, what is the cause of our separation from God and our need for reconciliation?

The cause of our separation is disobedience. Eve was tempted to sin by a desire to have knowledge of good + evil AND that the fruit looked good to eat. So, the 1st is prideful and the 2nd is sensual.

---

[3] Saint Teresa of Avila, *The Way of Perfection*, as translated in *The Collected Works of St. Teresa of Avila*, vol. 2, 126.

b. Why didn't God just cancel out our debt rather than sending His Son to die for our sins?

Perhaps so we as human beings have an example to imitate - He could have done anything.

c. What does this say about the justice of God and the origin of this virtue?

God's justice is not the same as man's b/c in human terms only the guilty should suffer not the innocent.

d. What should be our response to so great a gift?

Desire to please God always

Woman of Justice: The Poor Widow

Read Luke 21:1-4. These verses tell us the short yet memorable story of "the widow's mite."

1. Why does Jesus commend the poor woman's giving? What does she do that is noteworthy, and how does this compare with the others who gave?

Jesus commends her b/c she made a sacrifice whereas the others gave out of their abundance

2. How is generosity related to the virtue of justice?

To give another their due often will require one to be generous and to give of themselves not just from their abundance.

3. Aside from financial contributions, in what areas of our lives can we be generous with God?

Time is the most valuable - service to neighbor - more time spent in prayer or service - more time reading spiritual works

4. Of the things you listed in response to question 3, which of these can you offer to God more generously? How will you practically and prayerfully implement your ideas?

I will make a special effort each day to take opportunities presented by the children or my husband to put down things I want to do and rather, do something for them.

Memory Verse

"For our sake he made him to be sin who knew no sin,
so that in him we might become
the righteousness of God."
2 Corinthians 5:21

For example, if one of the children ask me to read/color/play and I have something else that I would rather do, I will put off my desire + serve first.

Courage

"By your endurance you will gain your lives."
Luke 21:19

Christian tradition tells us that all of the apostles, except Saint John, were killed because of their witness to Jesus Christ. Eusebius, an early Christian historian, has written that Saint Peter was crucified and Saint Paul was beheaded, both by the order of the Roman Emperor Nero in the first century. At the end of the first century, the Roman Emperor Domitian organized a fierce persecution of Christians living in the Empire. The reason: Christians refused to offer sacrifices to Domitian as a god. They would soon face the same fate as the apostles. These martyred men and women bore witness to the power and authenticity of their faith by a courage that enabled them to face death and pass through it to the gates of heaven.

It is an ironic fact of history that, while the persecution of Christians raged, the number of Christians grew in leaps and bounds. Only two generations after Jesus selected twelve men to preach the Gospel and baptize, there were more than 500,000 Christians in the Roman Empire.

Fortitude—commonly called courage—is the virtue that has not only helped Christians become martyrs, but also has transformed sinners into saints. The virtue of courage enables us to feel and cope with our fears of physical, spiritual, and emotional suffering so that we can do the will of God even in the face of our fears. Just as a martyr needs the virtue of courage in his or her hour of trial, so too does the sinner who is striving to become a saint. Courage is necessary not only in the "lion's den," but also in the home, supermarket, and even when facing ourselves. Fortitude is an eminently practical virtue.

"Death, but not sin!"[1]

Saint Dominic Savio (1842-57)

1. Using the brief history lesson above and perhaps your dictionary, what is courage?

Courage is the ability to face fear + act properly in spite of fear.

2. What do the following verses add to our understanding of courage?

a. Proverbs 28:1 *Being righteous helps us to have courage*

b. Philippians 1:27-28 *You will be saved if you stand up to your opponents + strive to do good*

c. 2 Timothy 1:7

3. Why is courage an important virtue for a Christian, and how is it useful?

Courage enables us to admonish one another and to be an example to others that the things of heaven matter more than those of earth.

---

[1] Jill Haak Adels, ed., *The Wisdom of the Saints* (New York: Oxford University Press, 1989), 149.

"If thou wilt observe the virtues of fortitude and perseverance, these virtues are proved by the long endurance of the injuries and detractions of wicked men, who whether by injuries or by flattery, constantly endeavour to turn a man aside from following the road and the doctrine of truth."[2]

Saint Catherine of Siena

4. Enduring suffering for the sake of the Cross is an important part of the Christian way of life. It is by the virtue of courage that we face and endure suffering. What do the following Scripture texts tell us about the purpose of suffering and the corresponding need for bravery?

a. 2 Corinthians 4:16-18 *to prepare us for eternal life + for the "things unseen"*

b. Colossians 1:24 *St. Paul is saying that we should rejoice in our sufferings b/c it makes up for something lacking in the church*

c. 1 Peter 2:21 *to unite our suffering to Christ's + follow his example*

d. 1 Peter 4:12-13 *Rejoice as you suffer so you may rejoice with Christ in glory*

"I believe that the great Polish poet Cyprian Norwid had this in mind when he expressed the ultimate meaning of the Christian life in these words: 'Not with the Cross of the Savior behind you, but with your own cross behind the Savior.' There is every reason for the truth of the Cross to be called the Good News."[3]

Pope John Paul II

[2] Saint Catherine of Siena, *The Dialogue*, as reproduced in *Treasury of Catholic Wisdom*, ed. John A. Hardon, S.J. (New York: Doubleday, 1987), 354.
[3] Pope John Paul II, *Crossing the Threshold of Hope*, ed. Vittorio Messori, trans. Jenny and Martha McPhee (New York: Alfred A. Knopf, 1994), 224.

5. The virtuous person exercises all of the virtues—not only a few. This is so because the virtues build and rely upon one another. Which of the other cardinal virtues is needed in order to be courageous? Why? Look up 2 Timothy 3:10-15 to check your answer.

I would say justice because to have courage in suffering one must appreciate that we are not "owed" anything – that we are only getting our "due".

6. Read Luke 21:10-19. What is endurance? How will endurance help us to gain our lives?

Endurance is the ability to withstand persecution and remain faithful to God's teachings – we will gain eternal life in doing this b/c they can kill the body but not the soul.

Because Luke has already said in verse 16 that some would be put to death, what does he mean in verse 19 when he writes that they will "gain their lives"?

Losing your body for the sake of faith in God gains you heaven + eternal life with God.

Do you think that endurance is another important aspect of courage? Why?

Endurance is key because suffering doesn't happen all at once – it is usually slow & drawn out.

7. While fortitude will help us conquer difficult situations in our lives, it also has a fundamental role in our spiritual lives. Saint Teresa of Avila has said, "I assert that an imperfect human being needs more fortitude to pursue the way of perfection than suddenly to become a martyr."[4] Why would a

---

[4] Saint Teresa of Avila, *Autobiography*, 31, 18, as quoted in Josef Pieper, *The Four Cardinal Virtues*, 137.

person need more courage to pursue perfection than to face death? What is it about our pursuit of holiness that requires so much courage?

More courage is needed to pursue perfection because it is a slow process that can easily cause someone to lose heart.

8. What do the following scriptural passages teach us about the role of courage in our pursuit of holiness?

a. Matthew 6:14-15 'Forgive others a God will not forgive you

b. Mark 9:35 To be 1st you must be last + servant of all

c. Luke 9:23-26 Take up your cross + follow me

"The Christian who dares to take the leap into darkness and relinquishes the hold of his anxiously grasping hand, totally abandoning himself to God's absolute control, thus realizes in a very strict sense the nature of fortitude; for the sake of love's perfection he walks straight up to dreadfulness; he is not afraid to lose his life for Life's sake; he is ready to be slain by the sight of the Lord ('No man beholdeth me and liveth'—Exodus 33:20)."[5]

Josef Pieper

---

[5] Josef Pieper, *The Four Cardinal Virtues*, 137.

9. It takes a lot of courage to face our sins and weaknesses. Is God calling you to demonstrate greater courage in your spiritual life? What is going to be your first step?

To get a good examination of conscience + try to familiarize myself + to pray it every day

Woman of Courage: Queen Esther

The Book of Esther narrates the story of a Jewish girl named Esther who would become the queen of a Gentile kingdom. It came to pass that the opening for the position of queen was made available thanks to the disobedience of her predecessor. When the king sought a new queen, Esther was brought before the king with the other young virgins. She was the adopted daughter of Mordecai, who served in the king's court. Mordecai asked her not to tell anyone that she was his daughter and therefore no one knew that she was a Jew. When Esther was brought to the king, he loved her more than all the other women and he made her his queen. The king also promoted a man named Haman, and commanded that all bow down to him. Esther's father, Mordecai, refused. Haman, enraged at Mordecai, and knowing that he was a Jew, decided to destroy all the Jews in the kingdom. Haman, an ancient-day Hitler, convinced the king to sign an edict demanding the annihilation of the Jews. However, God protected His people through the courage of Esther. By the wise intervention of Esther, Haman became a victim of his own edict and was executed while the Jews were spared. Read Esther 4:1-17 and 15:1-16, 3-15,[6] which describe Esther's courage.

---

[6] The organization of Esther is confusing. This is because Saint Jerome, in writing the Vulgate, separated the Greek and Hebrew sections of the Book of Esther,

1. What does Mordecai ask Esther to do, and how does she initially respond (4:8-11)?

To go to the King and ask him to spare her people - At first she says that the King will kill her

2. How does Esther respond to Mordecai's second request (4:13-17)?

She asks them to fast (+ pray) as she and her maids will to prepare

3. How does Esther 15:1-15 describe Esther's fear of the king and her task?

Although she was all dressed perfectly she was very fearful - she thought the King was "terrifying"

4. Why is Esther a model of courage?

Esther faced her earthly fear and chose to confront the King even though he could kill her. She relied totally on God - her "SAVIOR".

Memory Verse

"[F]or God did not give us a spirit of timidity
but a spirit of power and love and self-control."
2 Timothy 1:7

---

breaking up the narrative order of the story. The RSV has reordered the parts of the story according to narrative order, but did not change Saint Jerome's numbering of the chapters and verses, which is why the book is in its present form.

Self-Control

"For if you live according to the flesh you will die,
but if by the Spirit you put to death
the deeds of the body you will live."
Romans 8:13

Most people would agree that we are a society spinning out of control. Drunkenness, fornication, gluttony, adultery, rage, and general self-absorption permeate our world and are even glamorized in our entertainment industries. We are hard-pressed to find a magazine, movie, or television show, even during the so-called "family hour," that does not attempt to entice the audience by appealing to the base instincts of our fallen human nature.

Unfortunately, the same problems that plague today's culture often plague our personal lives. In fact, we probably do not need to look further than our delayed reaction to our morning alarm, our frustration with our children's slowness at getting dressed for the day, or the abundance of food set out on our breakfast table. We need more self-control.

The virtue of temperance or self-control is the one virtue that directs our attention inward. While the other virtues deal with our interaction with others, the virtue of self-control helps us order our personal lives. We need the virtue of self-control to get a handle on the many drives and desires of our lives that seem so unmanageable. Self-control helps us as Christians to order our desires in keeping with the truths of our faith.

1. Have you ever felt out of control or outmuscled by your passions? Why do you think it is such an unpleasant feeling?

In my daily work as a mother + wife, when one of the children do something unexpected - anger/frustration is the natural result.

2. In a society out of control, the definition of self-control is blurred. In your own words, describe self-control and why you think it is important.

Self-control is the ability to remain peaceful + focused no matter what is occuring around me. It is important in order to practice the other virtues.

3. Read Galatians 5:16-24. How does self-control, one of the fruits of the Spirit, help us to overcome the "works of the flesh"? Why is it important to overcome the works of the flesh?

Self-control enables us to overcome "works of the flesh" by keeping our focus on eternal matters, not the physical desires we have that come + go. ② They can keep us from making good decisions.

"To live well is nothing other than to love God with all one's heart, with all one's soul and with all one's efforts; from this it comes about that love is kept whole and uncorrupted (through temperance)."[1]

Saint Augustine

---

[1] As quoted in Catechism, no. 1809.

4. Read Romans 6:11-23. In these verses, what is Saint Paul exhorting the believer to do and how? What will be the result?

Do not be ruled by sin but be righteous.
If you do this, sin will have no hold on you—
only Gods grace will be with you.

"Therefore those who are perfectly obedient rise above themselves and take control of their selfish sensuality."[2]

Saint Catherine of Siena

Self-control is necessary to moderate those things that are good when used to preserve our lives, yet become evil when they are abused. It really is possible to have too much of a good thing. Our survival depends upon food, drink, and sexuality. Yet these three primal areas of life are the most difficult to control. They require the virtue of self-control if they are to be properly and healthfully used for our good.

5. Scripture clearly and unequivocally denounces both drunkenness and gluttony. According to the following verses, why should we be moderate in what we eat and drink?

a. Isaiah 5:11-12

b. Romans 13:11-14 *b/c salvation is near + in this way*
we can put on Christ

c. Ephesians 5:18
"Be filled with the Spirit"—(If you drink to much
you will not be

d. 1 Peter 4:7   *fill. of Spirt)*

because the end of all
things is at hand OR we do not know when we
will die

---

[2] Saint Catherine of Siena, *The Dialogue*, trans. Suzanne Noffke, O.P (New York: Paulist Press, 1980), 342.

6. The Church, by referring to sexual relations as the "marital act," has clearly indicated the proper context for such behavior. The Church teaches this in accord with Scripture. How do the following passages define the context and purposes of the marital act and the gravity of the offenses against chastity?

As members of Christ's body, we cannot defile Christ by mis-using our body.

a. 1 Corinthians 6:15-20

b. 1 Thessalonians 4:3-5 *to offend chastity is to be like those who do not know God*

c. Hebrews 13:4

Marriage must be held in honor

7. How does the uncontrolled use of alcohol, food, and sex affect us (see Romans 6:17-18)? How do you view the commands given us by God that prohibit their abuse?

Clearly, these commands are for our own good so that we are able to get to heaven as we were created to do.

8. How does our culture evaluate gluttony, drunkenness, and fornication? Has your understanding of these things been shaped by the Church? Do you need to change your thinking, and possibly your habits?

The culture is not supportive of any restrictions that help us to attain holiness. There is a natural aversion to these sins though that is bolstered by the Church.

Woman of Self-Control: Anna, the Prophetess

Read the brief but notable account of the life of Anna, the prophetess in Luke 2:36-38.

1. Anna was probably widowed as a young woman. How does she spend her days after the passing of her husband?

Worshipping God with prayer + fasting AND talking to people about God.

2. How does Anna model the virtue of self-control?

I think by her diligence in prayer and especially by fasting.

3. What does the practice of the virtue of self-control ultimately enable Anna to do?

To share God with others.

She is able to hear the Holy Spirit.

4. Prayer and fasting are tried and true methods of growing in holiness. How can you practically incorporate more of these basic Christian practices in your life?

Fasting would be beneficial to me. Perhaps I could start by fasting from snacks during the afternoon at night.

5. How would you benefit from having more self-control? Ask the Lord to help you and Anna to pray for you.

More self-control when it comes to snacks would be helpful for me. I tend to eat something enjoyable when I have the feeling of wanting it.

"For if you live according to the flesh you will die,
but if by the Spirit you put to death
the deeds of the body you will live."
Romans 8:13

Faith

*"And without faith it is impossible to please him.
For whoever would draw near to God
must believe that he exists and
that he rewards those who seek him."*
Hebrews 11:6

The Apostles' Creed and the Nicene Creed open with the powerful words, "I believe" and "We believe." It is interesting that the wording is not "I assert" or "I think," but rather a firm "I believe." The creeds emphatically summarize our faith, what it is that we believe.

Faith is the first of the theological virtues and a gift of grace from God. After we receive the gift of faith at our Baptisms, we have to choose whether or not we will accept it. As always, God offers us His good gifts, but never forces us to accept them. If we do accept God's gift of faith, and turn our hearts towards Him, we give Him the opportunity to transform our lives into something beautiful for Him (cf. Catechism, nos. 153-65).

1. Faith is one of those words that seem to take on a life of their own. What is faith? Compare your understanding of faith with the definition found in Hebrews 11:1.

Faith is the belief that God exists & created us to know, love + serve him.

Belief is that which we cannot see.

"Believing is an act of the intellect assenting to the divine truth by command of the will moved by God through grace."[1]

Saint Thomas Aquinas

2. Do you ever feel the need to justify your faith? Do you ever feel that in some way you are of lesser intelligence or don't have a sound mind because you believe by faith what you can't prove solely by reason and experience? Why or why not? What do you think is the cause of your situation?

No, on the contrary, I think it takes a stronger, more "hardworking" person to struggle and pray & think out our role in God's plan.

"In seeking him they find him, and in finding they will praise him. Lord, I would seek you, calling upon you—and calling upon you is an act of believing in you. You have been preached to us. My faith, Lord, calls upon you. It is your gift to me. You breathed it into me by the humanity of your Son, by the ministry of your preacher."[2]

Saint Augustine

3. Because faith has its source in God and it is a gift from God, it must bear fruit. What are the benefits of faith for the believer according to the following verses?

a. Ephesians 2:8 *You will be saved by faith*

b. Colossians 2:12 *You will be "raised with Christ"*

---

[1] As quoted in Catechism, no. 155.
[2] Saint Augustine, *Confessions*, 3.

c. 1 Peter 1:3-5 *you will receive a pure, undefiled inheritance in heaven*

d. Hebrews 11:6

To please God we must believe in him and that he rewards those who seek him.

"Faith is a gift from God. Without faith, no life is possible. For our work to bear fruit, for it to belong to God alone, it must be founded on faith. Christ has said, 'I was hungry, naked, sick, homeless. . . . You did it for me' (see Mt. 25:35-40). Our work is founded on faith in these words of Christ. Faith is scarce nowadays because selfishness is quite abundant; personal advantage is sought about all. Faith cannot be genuine without being generous. Love and faith go together; they complement each other."[3]

Mother Teresa of Calcutta

4. Rich Mullins, a popular Christian songwriter, calls faith without works "as useless as a screen door on a submarine."[4] How do the following passages explain the importance of good works as a way of expressing our faith?

a. Matthew 25:34-40 *By doing the physical works of mercy, we will be saved + go to heaven.*

b. John 15:1-11 *Only those who bear fruit will be pruned and saved - the others will be cast away.*

c. Romans 2:13 *"Not hearers of the law, but doers" will be justified.*

d. James 2:14-23

It does no good to say you have faith but another person is in need.

[3] Mother Teresa, *Heart of Joy*, ed. Jose Luis Gonzalez-Balado (Ann Arbor: Servant Books, 1992), 135.
[4] Rich Mullins, *Screen Door* (BMG Songs, 1986).

5. What are some practical ways you can live your faith in your daily life? What are some good works you can do?

To do things which will not be seen by another person – truly hidden deeds that God alone will see. (For A., and the kids)

"Oh Lord, let me know you that I may love you, because I do not want to know you except that I may love you."

Saint Francis of Assisi

6. In faith we are given the supernatural ability to believe what we cannot completely understand by the unaided powers of our mind. What are the benefits of seeking to better understand the mysteries of our faith?

a. Matthew 11:29

Our burden will be light

b. John 8:31-32

You will know the truth + the truth will set you free

c. Colossians 3:9-10

d. Romans 12:2

"Faith *seeks understanding*."[5]

Saint Anselm

---

[5] As quoted in *Catechism*, no. 158, original emphasis.

"I believe, in order to understand; and I understand, the better to believe."[6]

Saint Augustine

7. Faith is the virtue that enables us to believe what we do not see, based on the credible testimony of someone else. We cannot prove what we believe, but we believe that it is true because we trust the reliability of the one who told us. According to the following texts, why can we be confident that our Christian faith is true?

a. John 17:17 *"God's word is truth"*

b. 1 Timothy 3:14-15 *Has to believe in God's household deeds are evidence of faith?*

c. 2 Timothy 3:14-17
All Scripture is inspired by God + profitable for training in righteousness.

8. Read Romans 1:18-25. According to Saint Paul, is it possible for all to believe in God? Why have some failed to believe?

Yes it is - some failed bk they become futile in their thinking + exchanged the Creator for a creature.

9. We are obligated to "nourish and protect our faith" (Catechism, no. 2088). How can we nourish our faith? Protect it?

Nourish it by reading + surrounding ourselves with holy things / Protect it by not allowing ourselves to fall into occasions of sin.

---

[6] Ibid.

Woman of Faith: Elizabeth

The Catechism (no. 165) tells us that when our faith is tested, we should look to the witnesses of faith. The first chapter of Saint Luke's Gospel tells us of a barren woman, remarkable in faith, familiar to all as the cousin of Mary. Read Luke 1:5-66.

1. How does Luke describe the spiritual lives of Zechariah and Elizabeth?

Both were righteous

2. How does Elizabeth respond to the prompting of the Holy Spirit?

She is grateful for the blessing of her child

3. What does Elizabeth say should be the name of her child? Why?

John bc the Angel Gabriel told this to Zachariah

4. How do the events of Elizabeth's life demonstrate her faith?

Even though she is older she is not distressed about having a child — she is grateful instead.

5. What lessons can be drawn from Elizabeth's life and applied to our own?

Welcoming children as the Church teaches - Not being anxious or fearful but to completely trust God to provide.

================ *Memory Verse* ================
"Now faith is the assurance of things hoped for,
the conviction of things not seen."
Hebrews 11:1

Hope

"*Let us hold fast the confession of our hope without wavering,*
for he who promised is faithful."
Hebrews 10:23

While spending a summer in San Diego, I went to Tijuana, Mexico. The poverty I witnessed while traveling through the slums of the city was incredible. I had never seen anything like it. It was like the pictures I'd seen on television and in magazines, except it was real—all too real. I learned that poverty exists, and not just in the glossy photos of a *Life* magazine exposé. It was much more awful than any picture could depict. A short while after my brief trip to Tijuana, I spent a day in the Los Angeles area with a group of friends. As tourists, we strolled down the "Walk of Fame" to see the Hollywood signs and gawk at the breathtaking homes in Beverly Hills. While in Beverly Hills, we decided to tour the famous Rodeo Drive and stop in a few of the elite shops. As we walked through the shops of the rich and famous browsing over $800 belts and $1600 hats, I couldn't help but remember those living in desperate poverty just a few miles to the south.

Ultimately, the extremes of wealth and poverty disgusted me equally. I reasoned that life could not be about what you have or do not have. If life boils down to material goods, why should the poor want to go on living? And if luxuries truly make people happy, why do the rich commit suicide at least as often as the poor? Material goods can't fill the void that only God can fill.

So what is life about?

Death. After we die, we will live forever in one of two places. Life is about preparing for a good and happy death. In order to consider death properly, we need the virtue of hope.

The theological virtue of hope is the virtue that makes us confident that God will do as He has promised. His most important promise is our salvation—life in heaven enjoying His presence in eternal happiness. He has promised us eternal life if we believe in the death and Resurrection of Jesus and persevere in our commitment to Him. When we hope, our pilgrim journey of life is given meaning and death becomes the doorway to eternal life.

1. Hope is the virtue that bridges the gap between the other two theological virtues: faith and love. Hope is intricately tied to faith as its source because we hope in what we believe. Hope looks forward to its goal—perfect love in union with God. According to the following verses, what is hope? How do the following verses describe the virtue of hope and its connection with the other theological virtues?

a. Romans 5:1-5 *Because we have faith - we can unite our sufferings to Christ - This will give us endurance so we can have hope*

b. Romans 8:23-25 *" But if we hope for what we do not see, we wait for it with patience."*

c. Hebrews 10:19-24 *Hope for eternal life is connected to love + good works.*

"Wherefore there is no love without hope, no hope without love, and neither love nor hope without faith."[1]

Saint Augustine

---

[1] Saint Augustine, *The Enchiridion on Faith, Hope and Love*, trans. J.F. Shaw (Chicago: Henry Regnery Co., 1961), 9.

2. After taking a close look at the meaning of the theological virtue of hope, how does the virtue differ from mere wishful thinking?

Hope differs because it is based on the revealed truth that we will have eternal life by loving God completely.

3. Hope, by its definition, looks forward to something. What is the object of our hope?

a. Romans 8:18-25 *the glory for which we were saved*

b. John 14:1-6

c. Titus 3:3-7

d. Revelation 21:1-4

> "If you read history you will find that the Christians who did the most for the present world were just those who thought most of the next. The Apostles themselves, who set on foot the conversion of the Roman Empire, the great men who built up the Middle Ages, the English Evangelicals who abolished the Slave Trade, all left their mark on Earth, precisely because their minds were occupied with Heaven."[2]
>
> C.S. Lewis

4. A deeper prayer life is the fruit of hope, and prayer nourishes the virtue of hope (cf. Catechism, no. 2607). In prayer we acknowledge God and our dependence upon Him, and look forward to eternal life. It is also true that the only way to grow

---

[2] C.S. Lewis, *Mere Christianity* (New York: Macmillan Publishing Co., 1960), 118.

in the theological virtues is by the grace of God, which we can ask for in prayer. How do the following verses encourage you to pray more?

a. Jeremiah 29:12-14

b. Matthew 7:7-11

c. John 15:7

> "Finally, just as little children learn to speak by listening to their mothers and lisping words with them, so also by keeping close to our Savior in meditation and observing his words, actions, and affections we learn by his grace to speak, act and will like him."[3]
>
>   Saint Francis de Sales

5. Magnanimity is the natural virtue by which we demonstrate our hope by "thinking big." A magnanimous person is one who aims high and is confident of God's ability to do the impossible. How do the following verses exhort us to be magnanimous?

a. Luke 1:37 *Nothing is impossible w God*

b. Mark 16:15-20

c. 2 Corinthians 12:9

d. 2 Timothy 1:7

---

[3] Saint Francis de Sales, *Introduction to the Devout Life*, trans. John K. Ryan (New York: Image Books, 1989), 81.

6. While hope is the virtue in which we, through faith and love, patiently expect eternal life, there are two vices that oppose the virtue of hope: despair and presumption. Despair says there is no hope—God *cannot* save a wretch like me. According to the following verses, why should we hope in God and not despair? How can a person be lured into despair?

a. John 3:17

b. John 17:1-4 *Jesus gave glory to God & asked him to see eternal life =>*

c. Galatians 4:4-7

d. Ephesians 1:11-14

7. The second sin against hope is presumption. If hope is patient expectation, and despair is the refusal to expect salvation, presumption assumes that our individual salvation is assured irrespective of our cooperation with God's grace. How does Scripture warn us against the sin of presumption and explain our need to continue in the hope of eternal rewards?

a. Matthew 24:13

b. Romans 8:24

c. Hebrews 6:7-12

How does the sin of presumption affect the actions of the
one who presumes?

_____

_____

How can we guard ourselves against this sin?

_____

_____

> "Now although such people are assured of a reward for perse-
> verance, they are not found to be certain of their perseverance.
> Can any man be sure that he will persevere to the end in the
> practice of righteousness, making progress in it? No one can,
> unless he is assured by some revelation from him who,
> according to his just but secret decision, instructs only a few,
> but deceives no one."[4]
>
> Saint Augustine

8. Hope is the virtue that enables us to look at death with
a proper perspective. What have you previously thought
about death and dying? What do you think about death
now? How will you change your life to reflect your new
understanding?

_____

_____

_____

---

[4] Saint Augustine, *The City of God*, trans. Henry Bettenson (New York: Penguin
Books, 1984), 444.

Woman of Hope: The Maccabean Mother

In the Book of 2 Maccabees we learn of an awful persecution of the Jews by the Greeks. The story sounds like the persecution of the early Christians by the Romans. The Gentile king decided to try to force the Jews to accept Greek customs, which would consequently cause them to defile themselves and deny their God. The writer of 2 Maccabees has included the story of a heroic mother and her seven sons' trial. Read 2 Maccabees 7.

1. Why is the king so enraged with the sons and their mother?

_____

_____

2. How does the mother react to the brutal torture of her children and how does she encourage them? Why does the mother react this way?

_____

_____

3. After watching the murder of six of her seven children, she is asked to persuade her seventh son to cooperate and spare his life. What does she do and why?

_____

_____

4. Why is this mother a model of both courage and hope?

_____

_____

5. Do you think your hope is as firm and exemplary as the Maccabean mother? If not, seek God's grace to grow in this virtue. What practical steps can you take to grow in the virtue of hope?

_____

_____

_____

Memory Verse
"He will wipe away every tear from their eyes,
and death shall be no more,
neither shall there be mourning
nor crying nor pain any more,
for the former things have passed away."
Revelation 21:4

Love

"For this is the love of God,
that we keep his commandments.
And his commandments are not burdensome."
1 John 5:3

One Sunday morning while attending Mass, I observed an elderly couple in the pew in front of me. The woman appeared frail and she seemed to be suffering from some form of dementia. I watched as her husband tenderly helped her up and down during Mass and attended to all of her needs, while she was obviously incapable of returning his favors with even a "Thank you." At the sign of peace, I overheard him whisper as he kissed her cheek, "I love you forever." She responded with a blank stare.

This man exemplified the power of love within the Sacrament of Marriage. He loved his beloved wife as Jesus does—heroically and unconditionally.

The virtue of love is the crown of all the others, as all the virtues flow from love and back to love. Love, also known as charity, is the beginning and end of the practice of virtue.

1. There is a lot of talk about love in the world. What is love? Give examples of both real love and false love. (See 1 Corinthians 13.)

Children → actions like diapers
books, feeding in a cheerful
way.
Love that is only expressed in
words →

2. While the world talks a lot about love, the Bible is able to give us God's explanation of this eminent virtue. How do the following verses explain to us what love is?

a. John 3:16

b. Romans 5:8

c. 1 John 4:16-19

> "O Jesus, I ask only for peace—peace and above all LOVE that is without measure or limits. May I die as a martyr for You. Give me martyrdom of soul or body. Ah! rather give me both! Enable me to fulfill all my duties perfectly and let me be ignored, trodden underfoot, and forgotten like a grain of sand. To You, my Beloved, I offer myself so that You may fulfill in me Your holy Will without a single creature placing any obstacle in the way."[1]
>
> Saint Thérèse of Lisieux

3. After reflecting on what God has shown us to be true love, why do you think we need grace to love as He loves?

b/c we always put condition on love→

4. God has demonstrated His love towards us in the sacrifice of His Son and in His continual outpouring of grace in our lives. According to the following verses, how are we to show our love for God?

---

[1] Saint Thérèse of Lisieux, *The Story of a Soul*, 101.

a. John 14:15-17

b. 1 John 2:3-6

c. 1 John 5:3

"The man who loves like this loves truly; and in so doing he loves the things of God. He loves purely and without self-interest, and so will readily obey God's pure command, purifying his heart in love's obedience, as Peter says. He loves justly, and takes this just commandment to his heart. This love, true, pure and just, he does not offer upon terms, and so it is acceptable with God. It is pure love, for it is shown in deed and truth, not merely in vain words. It is just love, because he freely gives who freely has received. Love of the quality of God's own life is this, seeking no more its own but those things that are Christ's, even as He sought ours—or rather *us*, and never sought His own."[2]

Saint Bernard of Clairvaux

5. How do the following verses express the need for us to back up our love for God and neighbor with actions? What is the reward for showing love to our neighbor?

a. Matthew 25:34-40

b. Hebrews 6:10

c. 1 John 3:17-18

d. 1 John 4:7-12

---

[2] Saint Bernard of Clairvaux, *On the Love of God*, as reproduced in *Treasury of Catholic Wisdom*, 198, original emphasis.

6. Examine your conscience and ask the Lord to reveal to you an area of your life in which you need to be more generous with God. How could you love God in a heroic way? Ask Him to help you know.

Woman of Love: Mary, Mother of God

"From the first moment of her divine motherhood, of her union with the Son whom 'the Father sent into the world, that the world might be saved through him' (cf. Jn. 3:17), *Mary takes her place within Christ's messianic service*. It is precisely this service which constitutes the very foundation of that Kingdom in which 'to serve . . . means to reign.'"[3]

Pope John Paul II

The story of the love of our Mother Mary is a stellar example of human love and we are wise to imitate her example. Read Luke 1:26-40.

1. How does Mary's response to the angel Gabriel, also known as her *fiat*, show us her faith, hope, and love?

---

[3] Pope John Paul II, Apostolic Letter On the Dignity and Vocation of Women *Mulieris Dignitatem* (1988), no. 5.

2. What sacrifices does Mary make to become the Mother of God?

_____

_____

3. How does God reward Mary for her love?

_____

_____

4. Why is real love always about service and sacrifice?

_____

_____

5. How is God calling you to imitate Mary more fully in your life?

_____

_____

_____

══════════ *Memory Verse* ══════════
"And walk in love, as Christ loved us
and gave himself up for us,
a fragrant offering and sacrifice to God."
Ephesians 5:2

Back to Virtue
→ by Peter Kreeft

LEADER'S GUIDE
GENERAL SUGGESTIONS

Thank you for offering your time and energy to lead this Bible study. It is a great privilege to serve the Lord by serving others. He who is faithful will reward your generosity. To help you get started, here are a few general suggestions for leading a small group Bible study.

1. How do you start a Bible study group? Simply ask your friends, colleagues, neighbors, and/or fellow parishioners if they would like to join you in a Bible study. Tell them what the study is about and when and where you would like to meet. It is helpful if you are able to meet at an agreed-upon time and place, preferably once a week in someone's home. Because this Bible study is designed to facilitate discussion, a small number of members is preferable. A group of five or six is ideal, but a few less or more would be fine.

2. You should cover approximately one chapter a week in one to two hours. However, some chapters may take more time depending on the amount of group discussion. Feel free to allow your group to take more time on the chapters when the discussion is edifying and productive. It is okay if a chapter takes more than one week to cover.

3. The atmosphere of the Bible study should be comfortable and non-threatening. It is important that everyone feels respected and is able to share her thoughts. You may want to provide refreshments or have group members take turns providing a small treat.

4. Each meeting time should begin and end with prayer. It is also a good idea to have members share their personal prayer requests and make a commitment to pray for one another throughout the week.

5. As leader, your job will be to facilitate and move the discussion along, as well as to correct any misunderstandings. You will want to prepare for the Bible study by doing the assigned chapter and preparing extra questions you will ask. The other members should prepare for the study time by completing the assigned chapter before they arrive.

6. Spend some time each week praying for the success of the Bible study and each of the women in your group.

Answers, Information, and More Questions

The second part of the Leader's Guide contains the answers to the objective questions, additional background information, and questions for group discussion. The answers to the questions are marked with an "A," suggested questions for discussion are denoted by "Q" and printed in italics, and "I" sets off any additional information. You may feel free to include or leave out any of the questions and information in your weekly study.

Lesson 1
Virtue Explained

1. Allow the women an opportunity to share their ideas.

I: A modern confusion over the virtues is related to a misunderstanding of what is good. One such misunderstanding comes under the heading of "moral relativism," which holds that whatever you feel or think is okay irrespective of objective norms. However, "the good" is an objective reality. See the chapter on Wisdom.

Q: *How has the philosophy of moral relativism watered down the practice of the virtues?*

2. Allow the group to share their ideas. Virtue is health of the soul because the good habits created by virtue preserve the soul from mortal sin and, therefore, spiritual death. The habitual practice of the virtues lead one to God which is the ultimate health of the soul.

3. A: The practice of the virtues (self-control, prudence, justice, and courage) is the work of those who love righteousness and nothing is more profitable than these. This work is profitable because it will increase what those who practice it love—righteousness.

4. A:
    a. These two verses exemplify Jesus' humility. The King of the Universe was born of a peasant girl in a stable and, from His infancy, He teaches us the necessity of detachment from earthly things and their pleasures.

b. Jesus was obedient to God the Father and knew that His fulfillment was in doing His Father's will. Our happiness and fulfillment is to be found in obedience to God's will for our lives and doing His work here on earth.

c. Jesus explained to the Pharisees that the greatest commandments were to love God and love our neighbor. We are to love like Jesus because love is the greatest of all virtues (cf. 1 Cor. 13:13).

5. A:

a. We are to be virtuous (cleanse body and soul) so to become holy out of reverence for Christ.

b. We need to be virtuous because God has destined us for salvation through Jesus who died for us.

c. When we fight the good fight and live virtuously, we will have our reward in heaven.

d. God calls us to live sober, upright, and godly lives. This trains us to reject worldly passions as we put all our hope in Our Lord Jesus Christ.

6. A:

a. Those who fail to conform their daily lives to the will of God are called evildoers and are denied entrance to God's kingdom.

b. If we do not practice the virtues and make a concerted effort, we run the risk of losing the prize, which is heaven.

c. These verses tell us the most basic of principles—what we sow, we will reap. If we sow good or the product of virtue, we will reap good; and if we sow evil or the product of vice, we will reap evil.

7. A:

    a. David was faithful in the little tasks he was assigned in life. Because David fulfilled his duty as a shepherd well and was faithful in the little details of life, he was prepared for the major challenges.

    b. Allow the women an opportunity to share how they can apply this lesson to their own lives.

8. A: We are to seek all that is good by setting our minds on "things that are above," on God. We are to put to death immorality, impurity, passion, evil desire, covetousness, anger, wrath, malice, slander, and foul talk.

9. Allow the women to share their answers to this question if they are comfortable in doing so.

    I: As a leader, you may want to supplement your knowledge of the faith and the virtues through further reading. The following are titles I have found to be gems. You may even want to suggest them to the women you are leading for personal growth.

    <u>On the faith</u>: *Theology and Sanity* by Frank Sheed (Ignatius Press). I never tire of recommending this book. I love it! You will not be disappointed.

    <u>On the virtues</u>: *The Four Cardinal Virtues* (University of Notre Dame Press) and *Faith, Hope, Love* (Ignatius Press), both by Josef Pieper.

Lesson 2
Wisdom

1. Allow the women an opportunity to share their ideas.

2. A:
  a. We will be judged based upon our works. We need wisdom to do what is right.
  b. We will be judged on how well we treated others and whether we performed works of mercy as if for the Lord Himself.
  c. We will each give an account of our lives to God.
  d. We will each receive good or evil according to what we have done in this life. All of these verses discuss God's judgment of our works and the reward we will gain for them. We need to know what good we must do to inherit eternal life, and how to apply Christian principles to our everyday lives.

3. Allow the women to share their ideas.

In the second chapter of the Book of Wisdom, the unwise say that after life there is nothing, that the dead are simply food for worms, and so it is best to "live it up" while there is time.

Much in our present day revolves around materialism and the desire for pleasure and luxury.

4. A:
  a. The wise discerns what is right, is filled with the fruit of good deeds, looks to the future, is cautious and patient, avoids evil, and acquires knowledge.
  b. The wise man has foresight and protects himself from danger.

5. A:

a. We are to ask God, who will give wisdom to us generously.

b. The fear of the Lord is the beginning of wisdom.

c. If we seek wisdom, we should ask for it in prayer.

d. Wisdom is a gift that is given to those who love God.

6. A:

a. The Lord gives wisdom.

b. The Lord created wisdom.

c. God is the guide even of wisdom.

7. A:

a. The way to heaven is a narrow, difficult path.

b. We must imitate Jesus by serving others.

c. We cannot serve two masters. When we choose to serve God and seek righteousness, we can be confident that God will provide for us.

8. Allow the women an opportunity to share their ideas. You might want to discuss with them the negative effect of some television programs, movies, and women's magazines that offer repeated messages that glorify fornication, immodesty, and the masculinization of women. It will be important to add to the conversation the need to protect ourselves from unwholesome media and activities as an effective way of keeping focused on our goal of heaven.

9. A:

a. Those who "do" the law will be justified.

b. Whatever a man sows he will reap. We will reap eternal life if we continue in good deeds.

c. If we are "doers" of God's Word, we will be blessed in what we do.

10. Give the women ample opportunity to share their thoughts and ideas.

Woman of Wisdom: Judith

1. A: Her "heart's disposition is right"; that is the way Uzziah describes the source of Judith's wisdom. In other words, she loved God and sought Him as her source for everything.

2. A: Judith's first priority is prayer. In her prayer she praises God and seeks His power to bring success to her plans.

3. A: Judith dresses in her finest attire and uses her beauty and a lie to get to Holofernes. She prepares for her later escape from the Assyrians by getting them to allow her and her maid to go out late every night to pray. She also convinces them to allow her to have her own food bag. Finally, when Holofernes is passed out on his bed from drinking, she cuts off his head, pulls down his canopy, and returns to the Israelites with Holofernes' head in her food bag.

4. A: Judith tells the Israelites to come out of the city as if they were going to enter the camp of the Assyrians, and the Assyrians will flee when they realize that Holofernes is dead. They should "cut them down as they flee."

5. A: Through prayer and reflection Judith discerns what is the wise thing to do in order to liberate the Israelites. She uses the resources at her disposal, namely her beauty and intellect, to bring down the entire Assyrian army. Allow the women ample opportunity to share their ideas. You may want to encourage them to think about the way Judith clung to the truths of God's character, used her resources, strategized, and organized. You might also want to highlight the bravery with which Judith completed her plans.

Lesson 3
Justice

1. Allow the women an opportunity to express their opinions.

2. A: A human person was conferred special rights and dignity when he or she was made a person in the image of God.

I: To be in the image of God means to reflect His characteristics, albeit dimly.

Q: *Read the quote from Saint Augustine. What does it mean to "rest in God"? What does this quote mean to you?*

3. A:
   a. Not only are we not to harm our brother, but we are not to be angry with him or insult him.

I: The Glossary at the back of the Catechism defines anger as "an emotion which is not in itself wrong, but which, when it is not controlled by reason or hardens into resentment and hate, becomes one of the seven capital sins. Christ taught that anger is an offense against the fifth commandment." See also Catechism, nos. 1765, 1866, 2262, and 2302.

   b. We are called to respond to injustice with kindness.
   c. We are to love our neighbors as ourselves.

I: The commandments of Jesus, summed up in loving our neighbors as ourselves, require grace. They are not a simple exchange of what is due and a proportionate response for wrongdoing. Jesus tells us to go "beyond the call of duty" through the power of His love in us.

Q: *Consider the quote from Saint Thérèse. How can we learn to practice this "giving the benefit of the doubt" in daily life? What other spiritual lessons have you learned from this quote of Saint Thérèse?*

4. Allow the women the opportunity to share their ideas. Every day we encounter situations that require us to practice the virtue of justice. Smiling and speaking gently to a rude salesperson, refusing to steal office supplies or time from our employer by a neglect of duties, and even prioritizing our lives—putting God and our family first—are practical ways that we live Jesus' standards of justice in our daily lives.

5. A:

	What do we owe God?	**How do we pay our debt?**
Matthew 6:24	undivided devotion and service	frequent sacraments, prayer, service to neighbor
Mark 12:32-33	love God with all our heart and neighbors as ourselves	Mass, prayer, sacrificial service: visit the sick, make meals for home-bound, etc.
1 Samuel 15:22	obedience	obey the Ten Commandments and moral precepts of the Church, all for the love of Christ

I: Catechism, no. 2095 teaches us that the virtue of *religion* disposes us to give to God what we owe Him as creatures.

6. A:

a. God gave His Son as a sacrifice for our sins, and whoever believes in Him will inherit eternal life.

b. Jesus became the offering for our sins, and through Him we are made right before God.

c. By Christ's act of righteousness, we are made righteous.

7. A:

a. Pride is the root of all sin, most notably, original sin.

b. God is perfectly just at all times and therefore He could not contradict Himself and turn a blind eye toward our sin.

c. Our sin had to be dealt with appropriately in order for God to be true to Himself.

d. Our response to God's gift should be acceptance and gratitude shown in a life of love and service.

Woman of Justice: The Poor Widow

1. A: Jesus commends the poor widow's giving because she gave all that she had. The others gave more, but out of their abundance rather than out of their need. In the eyes of God, the widow gave more than any of them.

2. A: Generosity is related to the virtue of justice because, in being generous, we imitate God, who continues to lavish us with graces and gifts. Generosity involves going beyond what we are obliged to give, but giving freely and lavishly as Christians empowered by grace.

3. A: Our time, talents, resources, and bodies are the main areas of life that can be offered back to God in a generous way.

4. Allow the women to share their ideas.

I: There are many ways to be generous with God. Some ideas include volunteering at your parish or in your community, using the talents God has given you. Perhaps you can teach CCD, counsel at the local crisis pregnancy center, organize a woman's Bible study, visit the sick of your parish, help organize and/or maintain a perpetual adoration chapel, do the artwork for your church bulletin—offer your gifts back to God in a generous way.

As women, we are especially called to be generous with our bodies since we have been given the power to bring forth and nurture new life. We must avoid artificial birth control (the use of it is gravely sinful) and prayerfully consider our reasons for using natural family planning methods. We need to balance "responsible parenthood" with a God's-eye view of children: They are a reward from Him and "blessed is the man whose quiver (or home) is full" (Ps. 127:3-5).

Lesson 4
Courage

1. A: Courage, in its ultimate test, is readiness to die rather than to deny Christ or commit a mortal sin. As it applies to the daily struggles involved in the Christian life, it is the virtue that enables us to know and confront our fear and do the good for the sake of doing the good. When we are courageous, we feel fear and yet do not allow ourselves to be mastered by it.

2. A:
    a. The righteous are bold as lions.
    b. We are not frightened by our opponents.
    c. God does not give a spirit of timidity, but a spirit of power, love, and self-control.

3. A: Courage not only helps us withstand temptations, but it also "strengthens the resolve" to resist them and pursue holiness (cf. Catechism, no. 1808).

4. A:
    a. We need courage to look beyond what is seen to what is unseen and endure the afflictions that prepare us for eternal glory.
    b. We are able to suffer for the redemption of His people.
    c. We have been called to suffer because Jesus suffered and we are to follow His example.
    d. Suffering proves us worthy of Christ and heaven.

I: It is important to note that courage is the virtue needed to endure the suffering required of us. If we do not have courage, we will simply shrink away from the suffering offered us for the sake of our salvation.

Q: *Why do we so often shrink from the prospect of suffering? Why do people usually view suffering as a punishment from God?*

5. A: Wisdom is the prerequisite of courage. In order to be courageous, it is necessary to know the good for which one is willing to suffer, and that good can only be known through the virtue of wisdom. In 2 Timothy 3:10-15, Paul is encouraging his disciple Timothy to endure sufferings with the reminder of what he has been taught by word and example.

I: The virtue of courage enables us to patiently endure hardships for the sake of the good. Courage, however, is not exercised when one suffers for the sake of suffering or is reckless with life.

6. Allow the women to share their answers. You might choose to look up the definition of endurance in your dictionary. In verse 19, Luke says that those with endurance will gain eternal life. Saint Thomas Aquinas summarizes this passage by stating that "through patience man possesses his soul."

7. A: We need courage to persevere in our commitment to Christ despite the daily challenges and fears that confront us. Satan, our fallen nature, and worldly temptations are formidable adversaries that are overcome only with God's grace coupled with our courageous commitment to Christ.

Q: *What spiritual challenges have you faced that required courage?*

8. A:

    a. We are called to forgive one another in order for Our Heavenly Father to forgive us. Forgiveness is sometimes a very difficult task, especially when the wrong is severe. Sometimes it requires tremendous courageous to forgive and to seek forgiveness.

    b. We must be a servant and the last of all if we wish to be great in the eyes of God. Such humility requires courage.

    c. We must deny ourselves and take up our crosses daily. We must lose our earthly lives in order to save our eternal souls. We need courage to trust in God's promise of eternal life.

I: All of these verses call us to renounce our earthly lives and pursuits in order to gain eternal life. Courage preserves us from loving this life so much that we lose our eternal souls. Courage enables us to face the ugliness of our sins and selfishness in order to overcome it for our eternal benefit.

Q: *How can we practically put the virtue of courage to work in our lives in light of these verses? How can we forgive? How can we serve? How can we deny ourselves?*

9. If the women are comfortable, allow them the opportunity to share their thoughts. The edifying testimonies of our peers are great ways to motivate us to strive for virtue ourselves.

I: A thorough examination of conscience, taking note of our patterns of strengths and weaknesses, would be a first and courageous step in the spiritual life. Making a practical game plan, preferably with the help and accountability of a spiritual director, to address our weaknesses would be the next step. Finally, supported by the grace acquired through the sacraments and prayer, put the plan into action.

Woman of Courage: Queen Esther

1. A: Mordecai asks Esther to go to the king and beg for the lives of the Jewish people. Esther initially responds to Mordecai by reminding him that if anyone approaches the king in the inner court without being summoned they will be put to death, and that she hasn't been called.

2. A: Esther asks Mordecai to hold a fast for three days and nights with her and her maids. After the fast she would go to the king. She says, "If I perish, I perish."

3. A: Be aware that chapter 15 of Esther has two sets of verses, 1-15 and 1 14, and we are studying the first, beginning with the words, "On the third day, when she ended her prayer . . ." In these verses we are told that "her heart was frozen with fear," that the king was "most terrifying," and that, after the king looked at her in "fierce anger," she fainted.

4. A: Esther is a model of courage because she faced her fear and did what was right despite her fear. Esther was so afraid that she fainted and yet she still made her request known to the king.

Lesson 5
Self-Control

1. Allow the women the opportunity to share their thoughts and experiences.

2. Allow the women to share their definitions and ideas. You may lead them to a dictionary definition. The Catechism (no. 1809) defines temperance as "the moral virtue that moderates the attraction of pleasures and provides balance in the use of created goods."

Q: *What negative results have you seen in your personal life when self-control was lacking?*

3. A: All of the works of the flesh can be eliminated by self-control. The Spirit enables us through self-control to choose what we will think and do rather than be controlled by our passions. To the extent we have overcome the works of the flesh through the power of the Spirit, we belong to Christ, and to the extent we have not, we are still enslaved to sin and death.

I: It is important here to note that we must remain steadfast despite our failures. Through frequent Mass and Confession, prayer and mortification, and in the power of God's grace, we will put to death our sinful passions.

4. A: Saint Paul exhorts us to control our passions through the power of the Spirit of God. Our freedom from sin grants us our sanctification and eternal life.

5. A:

    a. Those who get drunk are cursed because, as a result of their drunkenness and lack of self-control, they fail to acknowledge the Lord.

    b. We are warned against making "provisions for the flesh" so that we may be prepared for the return of Our Lord.

    c. God commands us not to get drunk—it is a sin.

    d. Because the end is near, we should be sane and sober so we can pray.

Q: *In what ways have you failed to exercise moderation in the areas of food and drink? What can you do to keep these two areas under control?*

6. A:

    a. The marital act is only appropriate within the context of marriage. Fornication is a sin against your own body, the Body of Christ, and the Holy Spirit, of whom you are a temple.

    b. Not controlling our bodily passions is equivalent to being a heathen who does not know God. Lust is a sin against charity and chastity.

    c. Marriage is to be honored and the marriage bed kept pure: "God will judge the immoral and adulterous."

7. A: When we indulge in the passions of the flesh, we become slaves of our flesh. Living righteously is not boring. Rather, it is more fun than living "in the flesh" because we can then enjoy God's gifts in the manner they were meant to be enjoyed.

8. Allow the women to share their opinions.

I: You will want to provide extra support and guidance for women struggling in any of these areas. You should encourage anyone suffering from excessive use of alcohol or other drugs to seek appropriate counseling. It is important to remember that premarital sex is a serious (mortal) sin and should be stopped and repented of immediately. Adultery is also serious sin and the couple would likely benefit from Christian marriage counseling.

Woman of Self Control: Anna, the Prophetess

1. A: She spends her days in the Temple in prayer and fasting.

2. A: She dedicates herself to prayer and fasting. She has many options for her life, but she chooses to spend it in worship of the Lord. This entails a great amount of self control because she sacrifices a great deal. She also chooses to live many years without a husband, dedicating herself instead to the Lord.

3. A: She is able to meet the Lord and speak of Him to others.

4. Allow the women to share their ideas. I suggest scheduling regular times of the day and week for prayer and fasting.

5. Allow the women to share their ideas.

Lesson 6
Faith

1. A: Faith or belief is the firm acceptance as true those things we cannot see or prove.

I: It is important to note that as Catholics we believe that God has established a Church through which He teaches us the truths of who He is and how we are to live. There may be teachings we do not completely understand (e.g., the Trinity) or find difficult to obey (e.g., the Church's prohibition of contraception). However, as part of the virtue of faith, we conform our minds and wills out of an obedience of faith. We believe these teachings not because we agree (although we should), but because we believe Christ has established His Church to lead us into all truth. We believe the Church because we believe Christ.

Q: *Have you ever found yourself questioning the Church's position on moral issues or theological teachings? How does a proper understanding of faith answer your questioning?*

2. Allow the women an opportunity to share their thoughts.

Q: *How have you responded when your faith has been questioned? Did you feel equipped to respond to your questioner?*

3. A:
   a. Faith is the means by which we accept the grace of salvation.
   b. Faith is the source of salvation.
   c. Faith brings salvation and a wonderful inheritance in heaven.
   d. In faith we are able to please God and draw near to Him.

4. A:
   a. At the final judgment, our faith will be judged based on whether it was expressed in action.
   b. The parable of the vine and the branches demonstrates to us the need to "bear fruit" by doing good works or we will be cut off. Our works and obedience to the commandments demonstrate our faith.
   c. It is those who do the law, not just listen, who will be justified.
   d. It is by our works that our faith in God is proven. We show our faith in God by our works.

5. A: There are many good works that we can do. The corporal works of mercy (feeding the hungry, sheltering the homeless, clothing the naked, visiting the sick and imprisoned, and burying the dead) and spiritual works of mercy (instructing, advising, consoling, comforting, forgiving, and bearing wrongs patiently) are a good place to start (cf. Catechism, no. 2447).

6. A:
   a. When we learn from Jesus, we will find rest for our souls. We are refreshed in our daily commitment to Him.
   b. If we are steadfast in following Jesus, we will know truth and it will make us free.
   c. Our new nature is renewed in knowledge after the image of God.
   d. The renewal of our minds will yield wisdom.

   Q: *Have you ever sought to better understand the mysteries of faith? What are the joys you have experienced in better understanding the mysteries of your faith?*

7. A:

    a. Jesus says that God's word is truth.

    b. The Church is the "pillar and bulwark of the truth." We can trust that what the Church teaches us is true.

    c. Scripture is inspired by God, and God cannot lie.

8. A: Saint Paul tells us that we are without excuse because God has revealed Himself in all of creation. People fail to believe when they choose to worship and serve creatures instead of God.

I: We are obligated to "nourish and protect our faith." We can sin against faith by both involuntarily and voluntarily doubting the truths taught by the Catholic Church. The Catechism teaches us that voluntary doubt is a refusal to believe or hold as true what the Church has taught. Involuntary doubt occurs when we hesitate to believe or have objections that are difficult to overcome (cf. Catechism, no. 2088). We need to respond to our own doubts by attempting to find answers to our questions from faithful sources (not seeking out those who will simply agree with us even if we are wrong) and building on the truths we do know.

9. A: We nourish and protect our faith by frequenting the sacraments and asking God for an increase of faith. We can also foster the gift we have been given by filling our mind with the truths of our faith found in the teachings of the Church (magisterial documents, the Catechism, and many other good Catholic books and tapes), and in reading the Holy Scriptures and spiritual writings. We protect our faith by understanding it more and avoiding those things that will make us waver in it.

Woman of Faith: Elizabeth

1. A: They are righteous, blameless, and obey all the Lord's commandments.

2. A: Elizabeth trusts the workings of God and expresses her faith loudly. She believes that Mary is the mother of the promised Messiah ("mother of my Lord"), and unabashedly proclaims this truth with great joy. Elizabeth also proclaims Mary is blessed because of her faith in God's ability to fulfill His promises.

3. A: John. Zechariah must have communicated to her the experience he had with the angel Gabriel, and she believed the words of the angel.

4. A: She believes God could reveal to her His truth through the workings of the Holy Spirit. She believes that God was conceived in the womb of Mary. She believes the words of the angel Gabriel spoken to her husband.

5. A: Elizabeth's life was one filled with faith and hope. We can learn from her to be sensitive to the workings of the Spirit and to believe Him when He works. Her example teaches us to trust in the wonderful power of God to accomplish what He has promised.

Lesson 7
Hope

1. A:
    a. Hope is the virtue given us by God's love. It is a gift of God to believe in Him and be at peace with Him. Because of the gifts of faith, hope, and love, we hope to share in the glory of God in eternal life.
    b. Hope is looking toward that which is unseen and believing that what is unseen will be accomplished. Again, we hope because we believe God and know that He loves us.
    c. It is a firm assurance that what God has promised will be done. We hope because we believe and abide in God's love.

2. A: Hope is confident assurance of what will come to pass because it is based in faith and looks toward love as its goal. Wishful thinking is not based in anything other than our thoughts, and its goal is not union with God.

3. A:
    a. The object of our hope is our salvation and the redemption of all creation.
    b. In these verses Jesus tells the disciples about heaven. Jesus wants them to believe in His words and place their hope in the home He is preparing for them. The object of our hope is living in our home in heaven with God forever.
    c. Eternal life.
    d. Life with God in heaven. Eternal rest.

4. A:
    a. God hears our prayers and desires to reveal Himself to us.
    b. God answers our prayers. He is a loving Father who gives us good gifts.

c. We can be sure that God desires for us to hope in Him. This verse promises us that if we ask to grow in this virtue, He will give us the desire of our heart.

Q: *Consider the ways you spend your time and how that reflects your priorities. In the same way that we can know our priorities by looking at our checkbooks, so can we also know our priorities by examining our date books. How can we deepen and prioritize our prayer lives? A few suggestions include: reserve a "prayer block" of time and write it on your calendar, pray short aspirations throughout your day, and finally, remind yourself to pray with whatever reminders work for you—perhaps a blank Post-it note next to the phone will remind you to pray for whomever you will be talking to.*

5. A:
   a. God does even the seemingly impossible when it is part of His holy will.
   b. Jesus empowered His apostles to go and preach the Good News of the Gospel. This message continues to be spread through the power of His grace given to His ministers and preachers.
   c. The power of God in our lives enables us to overcome our weaknesses and do great things for Him.
   d. God has given us a spirit of power, love, and self-control.

6. A:
   a. God intends to save the world through Jesus, not condemn it.
   b. Jesus has the power to give us eternal life.
   c. God has sent His Son to redeem us and has adopted us as His children. We are no longer slaves of this world.
   d. We have been sealed with the Holy Spirit, who guarantees our inheritance of eternal life. All of these verses

express the promises and power of God to give us eternal life. A person can be lured into despair by believing the lies of the devil. Two effective lies of the devil that could lead one to despair are an exaggeration of our unworthiness and the need to "earn" our salvation.

7. A:
   a. This verse explains that we need to persevere in the faith to the end of our lives.
   b. Clearly, hope is not something that we see or have obtained, but a patient expectation rooted in the promises of God.
   c. These verses express that faith is demonstrated through actions and done because of our hope in the promises of God. If we presume that our salvation is already sealed and we have no need to demonstrate our faith, hope, and love, we may choose to be lazy in our prayer life and good works. We can guard ourselves against this sin by prayer and maintaining a true understanding of our salvation. Jesus has accomplished the salvation of humanity, but as individuals we must choose every day whether or not we will accept this gift of salvation and show our acceptance by living in the power of grace and obedience.

I: Presumption is the sin of false confidence. It negates the virtue of hope because it assumes to know for certain what can only be longed for with hopeful expectation. It can also be a misplaced confidence in God's mercy or our own goodness. Presumption rears its head in many forms in the modern world:

(1) "Once saved, always saved": This philosophy holds that once you have expressed to God your faith in His power to save you, the actions of your life will bear no consequence on your eternal destination. This form of presumption confuses

faith with hope. Scripture and the Church are quite clear that faith in God is demonstrated by our faithfulness to God and His commands. In fact, when Scripture speaks of faith it is often-times in the context of obedience (cf. Rom. 1:5; Jn. 3:16-21; Jas. 2:18-24).

(2) "Wishful thinking": This is the modern philosophy that asserts that God would not send anyone to hell or even that hell does not exist.

(3) "Pelagianism": This is the age-old heresy that holds that we can "earn" our way into heaven by our good works irrespective of God's grace.

8. Allow the women the opportunity to share their ideas.

Woman of Hope: The Maccabean Mother

1. A: The mother and her sons refuse to eat the flesh of swine, which is forbidden by Mosaic Law. To eat the flesh of the swine would be tantamount to denying God Himself. The seriousness of this situation and committing this sin would be like a Catholic committing a mortal sin to save his life, which we are absolutely forbidden to do. It is better to lose this life than to forfeit blessedness in the next.

2. A: She encourages each of them by reminding them that their earthly lives are a gift from God as is eternal life if they die for His laws. Verse 20 says that she accepts the death of her children "because of her hope in the Lord."

3. A: She appeals to him as his mother, reminding him of a mother's sacrifices, and asks him to accept death nobly so that she will be with him and his brothers in heaven. She has hope in God's power to make things right and to give eternal life.

4. A: She is a model of courage because she encouraged her children to remain faithful to God and accepted the consequence of their faithfulness—martyrdom—even though it meant the death of her children. She is a model of hope because hope is the reason she was courageous. She focused her mind and heart on the promises of God and reminded her children of them as they faced their darkest trial.

5. Allow the women to share their thoughts and ideas.

Lesson 8
Love

1. A: Love is a sacrificial gift of self. Real love is an offering of your time, talents, and body to what is good, true, and beautiful—namely God. False love is selfish and self-serving.

Q: *When have you experienced real love?*

2. A:
   a. God loved us enough to send His only beloved Son to save us and bring us to Himself.
   b. While we were sinners, Christ died for us. He sacrificed His life for us when we were seemingly unlovable.
   c. God has shown love by first loving us unconditionally. God is love.

3. Allow the women an opportunity to share their ideas. True love is impossible without the grace of God. Love, as God defines it, is difficult for us who are still selfish and have yet to be perfected in love.

4. A:
   a. We are to keep His commandments through the power of the Holy Spirit.
   b. We show God our love by obeying His commands and modeling our lives after the example He left for us to follow.
   c. Again, we love God by keeping His commandments.

5. A:
   a. God commands us to love our neighbor, which means caring for those in need. Those who perform spiritual and corporal works of mercy will inherit their eternal reward (cf. Catechism, no. 2447).

b. Our service to our neighbors is seen as service to God and will be rewarded in heaven.

c. We love God by caring for our neighbor, which will gain for us our heavenly reward.

d. If we show God our love for Him by loving our neighbor, we will gain eternal life.

6. Allow the women to share their ideas.

Woman of Love: Mary, Mother of God

1. A: Mary's response to the angel shows that she believes God's words are true and that she hopes to see their fulfillment. She loves God enough to overcome her fear and do that which is both sacrificial and difficult.

2. A: Mary risks her marriage to Joseph and possible death, if Joseph does not believe her that the baby is from God. As the Mother of God she is promised that a sword would pierce her heart (cf. Lk. 2:35), which it did as she watched her beloved Son hang on the Cross, unjustly killed.

3. A: Mary becomes the Mother of God and Queen of Heaven and Earth.

4. A: God is love and He is always serving and sacrificing for us. Through Christ, He has given us the example for us to follow (cf. Jn. 13:15).

5. Allow the women an opportunity to share their responses.

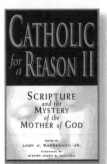

Diane - 882-4108